CLAUDIA PATRICIA MERLO

It's Sushi Time Somewhere

This book was professionally typeset on Reedsy.
Find out more at reedsy.com

Contents

My Son, Carlos Daniel Escobedo Loera, thank you for always going on silly Sushi adventures with me! You were my very first Sushi accomplice; you became The Great Wasabi Samurai because when it came to wasabi, man! You conquered the wasabi challenge! I will always treasure all those beautiful Takara Sushi memories. OH, by the way, I did not know then, but I have to break some hard news to you; rumor has it, wasabi is not real!... Yes, I know how you feel; I will explain all the truth in chapter three and reveal the secret.

I want to dedicate this book to my parents Aureliano Loera Ramirez and Mariana Garcia Lujan De Loera; without you, I would not be the human being I am today! To my brother Jesus Mauricio Loera Garcia, my accomplice in life and number one fan! Or so I say! And my amazing Husband, Kevin Merlo, for always being there for me and supporting my silly mind and mischievous and hyper personality. I love you all with all my heart; without you, I would not be the complete human being and happy person I am! Thank You from the bottom of my heart!

I am so grateful I found Publishing Life; it significantly gave a happy place to my hyper brain. Now I know where to put all my energy and feel very accomplished! Special thanks to the Mikkelsen Twins, Christian, and Rasmus!

Claudia Patricia Merlo

Introduction

W elcome to "IT'S SUSHI TIME SOMEWHERE." I was inspired to title my book by the famous American saying, "It is five pm somewhere" So, let us set up the tone and the ambiance by picturing this: it is almost 5 O'clock at the office on a regular weekday, and you hear from across the hall -Let's go and have some Sushi!- How did it make you feel? It doesn't have to be the weekend to get Sushi. It doesn't have to be a special occasion, right? IT'S SUSHI TIME SOMEWHERE at all times!

Where did your mind travel to with the sound of these five letters?
S U S H I!

Did you just have a Sushi orgasm? Man! All I know is that it will be Sushi Time soon! Your body knows it! Sushi touches your five senses! It is such a delicacy, a mystery, a pleasure; it is fun! It is family; it is friends, it is a date night, it is almost a sin! But why? Well, maybe we won't discover the answer to the why in this book, but we will learn some Fun Facts you probably have never thought about. If you are a Sushi lover like me, you will have as much fun as I did when I uncovered some fascinating facts about Sushi and Sake. I will also give you a couple of extra fun facts bonuses, so look for them. Come with me on this little journey, and let us discover together one fun fact at a time. I hope this book takes you away from stress and from too much life seriousness and genuinely give you an enjoyable time while going through this light read. I hope you have fun reading this silly-written book packed with actual facts.

Buckle up, and enjoy the Sushi Boat Ride!

Chapter One: Street Food

I s it true for you, as it is for me, that when you think about Sushi, you think about a very special occasion, better yet, a very glamorous special occasion! The image of a fancy restaurant or spectacular Sushi bar appears in your mind as a vivid image. When you go online to check the reviews about a few of your favorite Sushi restaurants, you will find many great comments accompanied by at least three money symbols typed next to the restaurant's name. Knowing that the places we like are highly rated gives us great satisfaction. Oh! And If we put the sound of the word "Sushi" plus the Japanese characters and sounds of the restaurant's name, added to how expensive the dishes are based on their website, all together make a significant and clear glamorous paint, it is almost like an expensive olio canvas we can't wait to go and experience! And, of course, the advice is to make sure you have a reservation ahead of time.

A voice on the other side of the phone says: "Your Reservation is set for seven pm this evening, Mrs. Merlo; we are looking forward to serving you, we hope you enjoy your visit, please let us know if you need anything from us, see you at seven"… As soon as we hang up the phone, we start getting ready for a beautiful outing. We take care of all the details because we have to match the occasion and show our glamour and fanciness, especially girls, right?

We get to the restaurant, and the main Sushi Chef, other Sushi Chefs, and the host or hostess shout in unison, "Irasshaimase!" We don't even know what that means, but we feel more important than a celebrity, thinking, "Oh! they know who we are!" We get situated, and immediately the happy chemicals start coming out of our brain and marching through our body! We take a deep breath and think this will be such a nice dinner and experience. Then we remind the host that our reservation is for the Sushi Bar. Of course, we must remind them of this because we must sit at the ultimate VIP Sushi bar where the chefs treat us like kings and queens. We place the fancy orders to start the evening: some seaweed salad with Kyūri (cucumber), edamame, tempura shrimp, two hot Sakes, and one Japanese beer. As the evening evolves, we place our main orders; mainly some specialty rolls and perhaps, an order of mixed sashimi. We enjoy the moment, talk about life, and fun topics, listen to the background music, check the ambiance, and take the whole experience in. We look around, analyze the Japanese decoration, eat some more, maybe we order an extra fancy roll, and to seal the night with a sweet note, we place an order of green tea mochi ice cream.

The Sushi outing is such a wonderful experience that we keep on talking about it the day after, we make comments about the chef's ability to cut the raw fish in such a delicate and artistic way, and we comment about how delicious the new specialty roll was, and we may order it again next time. Our subconscious is already planning to go back for another Sushi outing very soon! We comment on the excellent service and reminisce on the lovely company and beautiful experience. We notice that this location, in particular, has something magical, and you can feel the feng-shui; it is so inviting; we say, we will go back! All the stress went away, oh, and the valet gave an outstanding service. A deluxe gourmet experience! We shout at the end.

Now…let me take you on a time machine trip to many centuries ago. Close your eyes and imagine you are standing in a very busy farmers' market-like feeling on a street somewhere in South Asia. Let us imagine that the ocean is there too. If you have been to a farmers market close to the ocean, you can not only see the picture I am painting now, but you can remember the smell of the fish and shellfish, and you can also feel the humidity and the cool breeze. I am using watercolors now to give you the complete paint so you can compare it with the glamorous olio paint I gave you before. How does this comparison make you feel? One is warm, fancy, enjoyable, and expensive. The other feels cold, hustle-like, and a bit depressive, oh! And cheap.

Now sit down because I have to tell you some hard news…Sushi was street food! Yes, a dish associated with the poor and the working class. I am not saying that working class and working hard is bad, not at all! But, centuries ago work tasks were much more challenging because they did not have the modern features we have now. People would work insane hours until they almost drop dead. Our Beloved Expensive Glamorous Sushi was one of the few affordable staples back then for the hard-working and poor people. The fact is that Sushi was treated the same way we eat burritos and tacos from a taco truck or hot dogs at a city fair in today's times.

There you have it! Our First -Taco Truck-Like- unveiled Fun Fact: Sushi was Street Food!So don't feel too fancy and glamorous now! Ha ha..

Extra Fun Fact Bonus: Sushi was street food because real estate in Japan back in those days was unreachable for street Sushi vendors, but after September 1, 1923, when the Great Kanto Earthquake struck Japan, one positive thing came out of all the destruction. According to Thrillist, real estate prices dropped so low after the earthquake that Sushi vendors could afford more permanent locations. Sushi went from being served by vendors on the streets to being served by chefs in restaurants. Now, we can go back to feeling fancy and glamorous.

Chapter Two: Sushi, a delicious Japanese dish! Or not?

Let us picture ourselves when we are hungry but also a bit lazy to cook; we start thinking about where to go and what to get. We question ourselves what type of food craving we have at the moment…Mexican food? Italian food? Chinese take-out? Pizza? A hamburger? Or Sushi?… Most people who love Sushi, like me, would answer to our own question like this: "Sushi! Yes! Japanese Food sounds delicious right now!" At least, this is how I would have answered. Don't forget I put particular emphasis in "Japanese Food."

The very first time I was exposed to Sushi was at a beautiful Japanese restaurant on a mountain near San Jose, CA. I was around seven years old, and ever since, I have firmly believed that Sushi is a Japanese dish. Sushi started existing that day, at least for me. It was impacting to discover that it started centuries ago when people first wrapped fish in fermented treated rice throughout parts of coastal and riverside Eastern Asia as a method of convenient preservation. Hmm, I may try this method of preservation as a beauty recipe….Ok, let us continue…

Some authors and researchers have said that Sushi originated in South Asia between the 4th and 5th centuries BC to preserve fish in salt. Researchers believe that Narezushi, the original form of Sushi emerged somewhere by the Mekong River before it reached China.

Here we have our Second -Not Japanese- Fun Fact: Sushi did not originate in Japan! It originated in Eastern and South Asia. At some point, it reached China. Eventually, the Sushi we are more familiar with today came from Hanaya Yohei in Japan during the end of the Edo period around the mid-1800s.

Should I have said, "Yes, Sushi! Chinese sounds delicious right now!?"

Extra Fun Fact Bonus: Vinegar came over from China to Japan together with wine-making around the 4th or 5th century. Vinegar is indispensable to making Sushi and its origins come from Mesopotamia.

Chapter Three: What do you mean is not real, wasabi?

Remember I mentioned my first exposure to Sushi at age seven? Well, that also exposed me, or should I say "marked" me for life. I ate the whole green "thing" on my plate. I remember getting my plate and a portion of green "mush" on the side. I thought it was like a little bit of guacamole. Can you picture me after I swallowed the entire wasabi ball? I jumped off my chair and started screaming, crying, and yelling. The effect of the wasabi ball got to my head, through my nostrils, and got me crying for more than five minutes.

It never occurred to me to question what wasabi was made of, or what kind of evil veggie was this. I just learned it was a vicious, hot-spicy, "something" eaten with Sushi…Ok, I am over it and will turn the page now.

Throughout the years, I have learned to love the taste of wasabi! It goes wonderfully with all the Sushi rolls, the Sashimi, and the tempura. My knowledge about wasabi was: "All I know about wasabi is that it is green, mushy, spicy, and delicious."

Forwarding many years to now, my curiosity took me on a little research journey about the famous mushy green ball, and I discovered interesting information: Wasabi is a Japanese plant with a thick green root that tastes like strong horseradish and is used in cooking, especially in powder or paste form as an accompaniment to raw fish. When I was reading this, I nodded, supporting the information, and thought, of course! What else can it be? Dah!

I found that wasabi belongs to the Brassicaceae Family, also known as the Mustard Family and its scientific name is Eutrema Japonicum, from this point on I must refer to wasabi by its Royal Name out of respect, so let us all remember this name "Eutrema Japonicum" … This sounds very fancy. Sushi is a delicacy, and wasabi is too! So, I eat a delicacy on top of a delicacy! Superb!

I kept reading more about wasabi, and I got to a part that talked about the price, and I said…Give me one second, let me see what it says…"Wait, What?!" I had a shocking moment when I learned that the cost of wasabi is 250.00 dollars for 2.2 Lbs (1 Kilo). I thought: "No wonder Sushi is so expensive!" This must be because it belongs to a Royal Mustard Family, and It has to run a Royal Price. But little that I know, "Eutrema Japonicum" softly says to me: "Sushi is not that expensive because I am expensive. Eutrema Japonicum kept explaining that Sushi is not expensive because of her (the root). But, it is costly because it is considered a fancy, glamorous dish nowadays. And she (Eutrema Japonicum) continued explaining that wasabi (her artistic name) is not even present in those fancy dinners! Yes, I repeat, It is not even present in those fancy dinners because nobody can afford her cost! And from a business standpoint of view, it is not a good deal.

I made a very long pause—————(this is me, long-pausing)—————

I was rehearsing in my mind the last statement…"Wasabi is not even present in those fancy dinners because nobody can afford its cost"… .What????

And here's our Third -Sweet/Sour, very sour- Fun Fact: Wasabi, "The" wasabi we eat at the fancy Sushi restaurants is fake! It is made out of horseradish, sweetener, and food coloring. The real wasabi tastes nothing like the "wasabi" we get at the Sushi restaurants and Sushi bars, connoisseurs affirmed! And because it is that expensive, we won't see it at restaurants any time soon, so Fake wasabi will prevail.

….No additional personal comments on this one; I need a minute to recover from this unveiled fact… I am Not crying!

Extra Fun Fact Bonus: Wasabi and ginger are served together at Sushi restaurants; in modern times, people eat wasabi and ginger on top of each piece of the Sushi roll. In the past, ginger was used to preserve raw fish from contamination. The pickled ginger that usually comes with your Sushi isn't meant to be topped on your Sushi, but instead consumed in between bites of fish to cleanse the palate.

Ok, I get it, but I still like the flavor of ginger on top of my Sushi roll! So, there!

Chapter Four: No! Don't Trash the Rice!

D o you all know the meaning of Sushi? I always thought the word Sushi referred to the raw fish cut in such an artistic manner by the Sushi chefs. I thought Sushi was a combination of the ambiance, the Japanese beer, and the Sake. I thought Sushi meant raw seafood wrapped with rice to make a roll, but guess what? I just discovered that the word Sushi refers to the rice only, not the raw fish!

Rice Only - [soo-shee] In Japanese, the word Sushi means "sour rice" (the rice is traditionally moistened with rice vinegar).

Cut Raw Fish - [sa·shi·mi] In Japanese sashi, meaning "pierce" or "stabbing," and mi, "flesh" or "body.

Remember when we learn in a previous chapter that centuries ago, people wrapped fish in fermented treated rice as a method of convenient preservation? Well, everything sounded OK at that point; we all love the taste of the vinegary rice around the raw fish. If we ask for our favorite Sushi roll, it is in auto-mode that we picture the rice wrapping the ingredients inside! But…Let me unveil the next Fun Fact:

Our Fourth -Shocking- Fun Fact: When Sushi was invented, the rice was wrapped around the fish to extend its life, help create umami, a distinctly sour taste, and to protect it from insects. After the fermentation cycle was done, the rice was thrown out, and only the fish was eaten. The rice was discarded! Yes, discarded!

Extra Fun Fact Bonus: OK, now that humankind was able to save the day by keeping the rice, let me give you this extra fun fact. Traditionally, Sushi is eaten with hands, and I would like to quote a renowned Sushi Chef: "There is beauty in the process of the Sushi experience where it is made by hands, served by hands, and eaten by hands, so go ahead and use your hands." Masaharu Morimoto. Chef Morimoto prefers chopsticks for sashimi.

And here's my personal thought for this section, as long as the rice is present and not discarded, it doesn't matter if you use chopsticks or your bare hands to eat your Sushi rolls. Enjoy!

Chapter Five: The meaning of the word "SAKE"

⚜

I guess it is not the same to say "Goodness' Sake!" as "Sake is Good! Is it? Let us compare the two definitions for the sake of fun:

Sake /sāk/ noun: for the purpose of; in the interest of; in order to achieve or preserve.

Sake /ˈsɑːki, ˈsækeɪ/ In Japanese, the character Sake (kanji: 酒) can refer to any alcoholic drink, while the beverage called Sake in English is usually termed nihonshu (日本酒; meaning 'Japanese alcoholic drink').

On our fancy Sushi outings, we cannot skip the traditional Hot Sake, Flavored Sake, or Unfiltered Sake to pair with our "delish dish." So, since one cannot be without the other, this second part of "IT'S SUSHI TIME SOMEWHERE" will be dedicated to learning about this ancient Japanese alcoholic drink.

And now, for the sake of knowledge, let us dive into some Fun Facts about Sushi's best friend, S A K E!

Chapter Six: Sake is compared to beer. Not compared to wine?

OK, you all remember how much fanciness and glamour I have sprinkled here and there when I picture the ultimate Sushi Dinner Experience. So, let us go back to chapter one, where we were sitting at the VIP Sushi Bar, remember? Let us picture when the server came to take our drink order; we went ahead and asked for some of their NIGORI Sake and some of their Hot JUNMAI-SHU Sake. I don't know how you feel when you place your Sake order, but I feel so fancy when I do! I mean, Nigori? Junmai-Shu? It sounds like I know a lot and I have traveled the world! I say to myself, If I was at an Italian restaurant, I would be asking for their finest Cabernet Sauvignon, but since I am at a Japanese restaurant I will ask for their finest Japanese Rice Wine!

When my curiosity took me on this journey of learning more about my favorite food and pairing drink, I did a lot of reading, and I found out facts I could not believe because I had spent more than thirty years believing the wrong information. I don't know how to break it to you, yes, You Glamorous People, but here's the next Fun Fact:

Our Fifth -Brewed- Fun Fact: Sake has more in common with beer than wine. Here, in the USA, we often refer to Sake as "rice wine." Rice wine is made from the fermentation of rice, while Western wines are made from the fermentation of grapes. Sake is made from rice but through a brewing process. Yes! You read it correctly, Brewing Process. This is like making beer! The process is similar to brewing beer.

I will look for Sake on my next visit to the Beer Fest.

Extra Fun Fact Bonus: Sake is the oldest known spirit in the world. Some researchers think that Sake dates back to 4800 BC in China. Around 300 BC Sake arrived in Japan with wet rice cultivation. In the 1300s, breweries were built and allowed mass production of Sake. The industrial revolution brought machines that did the work the villagers' hands did once. And in 1904, Japan created a research institute to study the best means of fermenting rice for Sake.

Chapter Seven: Yeast in Sake? Beware Gluten intolerant!

Beware gluten intolerant! This was my first thought when I discovered that Sake is made with yeast. Yeast is an essential flavor ingredient! Yeast plays a critical role in Sake's quality. Each strain of yeast gives its own distinct characteristics of aroma and taste.

I don't know if you are familiar with the beer brewing process, but long ago I found out that Brewer's yeast, also called saccharomyces cerevisiae, is NOT gluten-free unless specified on the product label. Most brewer's yeast is a byproduct of the beer brewing process and contains gluten from the barley used to make beer. I enjoy beer, but I must be careful because it is packed with gluten. With this being said, when I found out Sake had yeast, my first reaction was "OH, No! I can't have Sake anymore! Because gluten really affects me." Then, doing more research, I found good news. I was thrilled to learn that Sake…..Well, let's go to our next Fun Fact to find the good news:

Our Sixth -Gluten FREE- Fun Fact: The four essential ingredients of

Sake -water, rice, yeast, and koji- are naturally gluten-free. The last ingredient, koji, sounds like it can be packed with gluten, but the good news for us, yes, us the ones who love Sake, koji in Sake is always rice-based!

All gluten intolerant like me out there, listen, we got lucky! Keep enjoying your Gluten-Free Sake! Cheers, Salud, Kanpai!

Extra Fun Fact Bonus: Sake has a higher alcohol content than either beer or wine. So, before going on a "Sake Binge," which means a period of excessive indulgence on Sake, have your Designated Driver or DD next to you at all times or take a taxi back home.

Chapter Eight: Secret Ingredient...Say What?

I must start this chapter with a disclaimer: "The Reading of this Chapter is at the discretion of the reader. This chapter is for adults only, and children must not be around. Some mental pictures after reading the information can be disturbing and life-altering. If you get nauseous easily, you should skip the chapter because what is read cannot be unread."

I am not going to elaborate much about this chapter with my personal stories, because thank God, I don't have any personal stories related to this secret ingredient. So let us go straight to the Fun Fact; maybe not so Fun, but here we go....Extra Buckle Up for this one:

Our Seventh -"Say What!"- Fun Fact: Spit, Yes! S P I T! Used to be a KEY ingredient! We learned in a previous chapter that today koji fungus is used to ferment the rice. But, long ago villagers would gather together to chew on the rice and then spit its mashed remains into a communal tub. The enzymes of their saliva aided fermentation.

OK, I am feeling a bit sick, let us think about some random things now so this effect goes away…Roses, Chocolate, Sunset, Soy sauce… I am OK now!

Random Extra Fun Fact: Don't dip that Sushi rice! Even though the soy sauce is served with Sushi, the rice is not meant to be dipped. It is frowned upon if the rice becomes drenched and starts to fall apart.

I hope this Random Fun Fact took you away from the spit trauma. But if this was not enough to help you unread what you read, let me take you to another Extra Random Fun Fact: Wasting soy sauce is disrespectful. Excessively using soy sauce with Sushi and having to throw out valuable soy sauce is highly discouraged. The proper way to enjoy your Sushi is to pour the tiniest amount and only pour more as needed, according to Trip Savvy…OK, I hope we can move on now!

Chapter Nine: No! Don't Pour Your Own Sake...Rude!

Picture yourself at a regular social function with your family or with friends. Have you ever thought about paying attention to "The Pouring Etiquette?" I never have! Because there is no Pouring Etiquette among my family or friends.

Could you picture yourself at your friend's house, celebrating some special occasion; then you feel like having a drink…As you talk to one of your friends, you walk towards the drinks section to make your choice. Then you decide you want to have a glass of Merlot…So, what's next? You grab the wine glass, open the bottle and pour yourself a Merlot. You keep on talking to your friend and walk back to the group to celebrate together and have fun!…… But for the purpose of SAKE and for our own sake, we must obey this Japanese voice that says: Rude! Don't Pour Your Own Sake! after hearing his voice, I must confront him (The Japanese Voice) and say: "What is rude about all I just described?" I can assure you that to me, to my friends, to my family, to us, here in America there is nothing wrong with it! But the Japanese voice will explain to me some Japanese facts I did not know about, and I will respect and follow from now on. Let us unveil the next Fun Fact:

Our Eight - "Don't Be Rude!"- Fun Fact: It is kind of rude to pour your own glass of Sake. Some say serving yourself suggests you don't trust your host to take care of you. Friends and loved ones use Sake to toast weddings, the New Year, birthdays, and other special occasions. So, pouring for a friend or family member—and letting them do the same for you—is meant to be an act of bonding.

OH, I got it now! I like this Sake Etiquette, and because of this, let us have a group hug!

Extra Fun Fact Bonus: Offer your Sushi chef a drink. If they accept, it is customary you take one with them.

Any excuse to have another drink, right? But Who am I to not have a drink with my VIP Sushi Chef? Kanpai!

Conclusion

This Sushi-Sake Boat Ride was something else! Wasn't it? It literally felt like I was on one of those roller-coaster adventure rides!

It took me from glamour to street food back to fancy restaurants thanks to an earthquake and a tsunami. Who would have imagined?

It shoot me straight to discover that Sushi is not originally from Japan, but I am glad that eventually made it there. Then this ride took me straight to a meltdown because wasabi is not wasabi, wasabi is fake! What? Can somebody lend me 250.00 dollars to get a kilo of the REAL wasabi? Ginger is to clean my pallet? What? I use toothpaste to do that. I am rebellious, and I will keep on putting it on top of my Sushi. I am so happy we are not trashing the precious rice in modern Sushi times and that Sake doesn't have gluten. I am a bit disappointed I can't refer to Sake as a rice wine anymore, but it is OK. I will see it now as a very fine Japanese Beer and I will gladly offer my VIP Sushi Bar Chef not only one shot of Sake but a few!

Irasshaimase!

Thank you so much for tuning in with me in this silly way of telling you some real facts about Sushi and Sake. I really hope you were able to relax, laugh, and forget about the seriousness of life by reading IT'S SUSHI TIME SOMEWHERE. I hope you enjoyed the Fun Facts about Sushi and Sake in this book filled with the silly flavor of the author, I would really appreciate it if you leave me a lovely and uplifting review on Amazon! Happy Readings! And I will see you soon:)

Resources

6 Interesting Facts About Sushi You Never Knew. (2019, June 3). Kobe Teppanyaki. Retrieved August 7, 2022, from https://www.kobeteppan yaki.com.au/blog/6-interesting-facts-about-Sushi/

Bento Asian Kitchen. (2017, October 19). 15 Fun Facts About Sushi. BENTO Asian Kitchen + Sushi. Retrieved August 7, 2022, from https://eatatbento.com/2017/09/15-fun-facts-Sushi/

sakowako.yum. (2015, May 2). 13 Facts You Probably Didn't Know About Sake. Retrieved August 7, 2022, from https://www.tsunagujapa n.com/13-facts-you-probably-didnt-know-about-sake/

Oxford Dictionary. (n.d.). Wasabi Meaning. Retrieved August 7, 2022, from https://www.google.com/search?q=wasabi+meaning&rlz=1C1 UEAD_enUS997US997&oq=wasabi+meanin&aqs=chrome.0.0i512j6 9i57j46i512j0i512l7.10125j1j7&sourceid=chrome&ie=UTF-8

Renton, A. (2018, August 18). How sushi ate the world. The Guardian.

Retrieved August 7, 2022, from https://www.theguardian.com/world/2006/feb/26/japan.foodanddrink#:%7E:text=The%20origins%20of%20Sushi%20are,%2C%20now%20Tokyo%2C%20in%201824.

Eat-Japan. (2017, September 2). Sushi History. Retrieved August 7, 2022, from https://www.eat-japan.com/Sushi-perfect/Sushi-knwoledge/Sushi-history/#:%7E:text=Sushi%20is%20said%20to%20have,of%20it%20in%20some%20parts.

Talk, H. K. (2022, July 14). Why Is Ginger Served with Sushi? (Solved!). Home Kitchen Talk. Retrieved August 7, 2022, from https://homekitchentalk.com/why-is-ginger-served-with-Sushi/

Dictionary.com. (n.d.). Definition of sushi. Www.Dictionary.Com. Retrieved August 7, 2022, from
   https://www.dictionary.com/browse/sushi

Thrillist. (n.d.). Thrillist - Find the Best and Most Under-Appreciated Places to Eat, Drink and Travel. Retrieved August 7, 2022, from https://www.thrillist.com/eat/nation/Sushi-facts-Sushi-trivia

Dictionary.com. (n.d.-b). Definition of sushi. Www.Dictionary.Com. Retrieved August 7, 2022, from https://www.dictionary.com/browse/sushi#:%7E:text=In%20Japanese%2C%20the%20word%20Sushi,flesh%E2%80%9D%20or%20%E2%80%9Cbody.%E2%80%9D

Beach, H. (2022, May 21). How an earthquake led to sushi being served in restaurants. Mashed.Com. Retrieved August 7, 2022, from https://www.mashed.com/870843/how-an-earthquake-led-to-Sushi-being-served-in-restaurants/?utm_campaign=clip

Wikipedia contributors. (2022, July 13). Sake. Wikipedia. Retrieved August 7, 2022, from https://en.wikipedia.org/wiki/Sake#:%7E:text=I n%20Japanese%2C%20the%20character%20Sake,meaning%20'Japane se%20alcoholic%20drink').

Puchko, K. (2017, January 17). 15 Things You Should Know About Saké. Mental Floss. Retrieved August 7, 2022, from https://www.mentalflos s.com/article/63105/15-things-you-should-know-about-Sake

E. (2020, August 4). Is Sake Gluten-Free? How to Find Gluten-Free Sake. Carving A Journey. Retrieved August 7, 2022, from https://www.ca rvingajourney.com/is-Sake-gluten-free/#:%7E:text=First%2C%20I% 20want%20to%20start,gluten%20depending%20on%20the%20circum stances.

Beyond Celiac. (2021, April 6). Is Yeast Gluten-Free? | Beyond-Celiac.org. Retrieved August 7, 2022, from https://www.beyondce liac.org/gluten-free-diet/is-it-gluten-free/yeast/#:%7E:text=Brewer' s%20yeast%2C%20also%20called%20saccharomyces,barley%20used% 20to%20make%20beer.

Saladino, E. (2021, May 19). Why You Should Never Pour Your Own Sake. VinePair. Retrieved August 7, 2022, from https://vinepair.com/ articles/Sake-serving-guide/#:%7E:text=%E2%80%9CThe%20traditi on%20of%20pouring%20for,Sake%20and%20conversation%20to%20 flow.%E2%80%9D